INSIDE THE LONDON CATACOMBS

TOP SECRET

MEGAN HARDER

Lerner Publications ◆ Minneapolis

For R.B. —Happy I5!
With special thanks to L.F.

Lerner Publications Company
An imprint of Lerner Publishing Group, Inc.
241 First Avenue North
Minneapolis, MN 55401 USA

For reading levels and more information, look up this title at www.lernerbooks.com.

Main body text set in Aptifer Sans LT Pro.
Typeface provided by Linotype AG.

Editor: Lauren Foley **Designer:** Athena Currier
Lerner team: Sue Marquis

Library of Congress Cataloging-in-Publication Data

Names: Harder, Megan, author.
Title: Inside the London catacombs / Megan Harder.
Description: Minneapolis : Lerner Publications , [2023] | Series: Top secret (Alternator books) | Includes bibliographical references and index. | Audience: Ages 8–12 | Audience: Grades 4–6 | Summary: "Buried deep beneath the outskirts of the city, the London catacombs are known for being as beautiful as they are eerie. Discover the London catacombs, including who was laid to rest there, why they closed, and more"— Provided by publisher.
Identifiers: LCCN 2022017761 (print) | LCCN 2022017762 (ebook) | ISBN 9781728476643 (library binding) | ISBN 9781728478357 (paperback) | ISBN 9781728485461 (ebook)
Subjects: LCSH: Catacombs—England—London—History—Juvenile literature. | Underground areas—England—London—History—Juvenile literature. | Burial—England—London—History—Juvenile literature.
Classification: LCC DA689.C3 H36 2023 (print) | LCC DA689.C3 (ebook) | DDC 363.7/509421—dc23/eng/20220629

LC record available at https://lccn.loc.gov/2022017761
LC ebook record available at https://lccn.loc.gov/2022017762

Manufactured in the United States of America
1-52245-50685-7/13/2022

TABLE OF CONTENTS

Form No. I
THIS CASE ORIGINATED AT

REPORT MADE AT	DATE WHEN MADE	PERIOD FOR WHICH MADE	REPORT MADE BY
	8/2/I9 : 9/2/I9		67c
	I/28/20 : 3/I2/2I,4/0I/22		
TITLE	I /5/22,		
		CHARACTER CASE	SECURITY MATTER - C

DESCENT INTO DARKNESS

A crowd of people dressed in black stood in lines
along the rows of wooden benches that filled the chapel.
They looked at a long wooden box on a raised platform.
The box was draped in dark velvet and surrounded by
white lilies. Inside, lay the body of their friend, neighbor,
or loved one. Slowly and quietly, the coffin began to move.

The coffin sank beneath the floor. It was going to the dim, chilly vaults hidden beneath the chapel. These vaults were the catacombs. The coffin would be placed on a stone shelf and locked behind an iron grate with other coffins.

The catacombs at Highgate Cemetery

CHAPTER I
GRAVE BUSINESS

Catacombs and graves line the path that leads to the main chapel in Brompton Cemetery.

Coffins were placed on shelves in the catacombs.

For a brief time in nineteenth-century London, catacombs were a popular place to bury the dead. Coffins rested neatly on underground shelves, locked away behind iron grates or stone panels. Loved ones who had passed on were secure from grave robbers and earthworms alike in the catacombs.

London built new cemeteries. But they would become crowded too.

Burial Crisis

Not long before this, burial was a messy business. In the early 1800s, London faced a burial crisis. The city's population was growing quickly. More people meant more deaths. The graveyards that surrounded the city's churches were overflowing.

People feared that these graveyards threatened public health. Shallow graves leaked smells of decay. Many claimed that the decomposing bodies were making the air and water dirty and causing sickness nearby.

To make matters worse, a new disease called cholera swept through the city for the first time from 1832 to 1833. It killed thousands of people. Cholera is caused by bacteria that spreads through infected water and food. But health officials didn't know that yet. Some people thought the stink rising from overflowing graveyards was causing the new disease. Was the burial crisis making people sick?

Burial Reform

Whether or not the burial crisis caused cholera, something had to be done. A movement began to reform the overcrowded

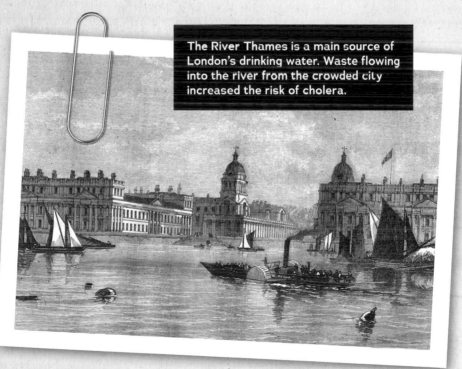

The River Thames is a main source of London's drinking water. Waste flowing into the river from the crowded city increased the risk of cholera.

churchyards. Other nations had solved their burial problems by creating new garden cemeteries, which have more open space than regular cemeteries. London officials followed this example. They laid out plans to build cemeteries outside the city where there would be plenty of space and fresh air.

Between 1833 and 1841, seven cemeteries opened outside the city. Together they were called the Magnificent Seven. They included Kensal Green, West Norwood, Highgate, Brompton, Nunhead, Abney Park, and Tower Hamlets Cemeteries.

SOLVE IT

A growing population and other changes led to a burial crisis in London. How would you solve a burial crisis? One way you could start is researching other ways to take care of the dead, such as burial in catacombs or cremation. Have options changed since the 1800s?

The Circle of Lebanon is a ring of tombs at Highgate Cemetery.

DECLASSIFIED

The decorations around the London catacombs could be seen as a spooky tribute or simple art. But the designs were chosen for their deeper meanings.

- Upside-down torches: A flame turned upside down will go out. But the upside-down torches on the gates to the Brompton catacombs are still lit. These torches represent the death of the body while the soul survives in the afterlife.
- Snakes: The Victorians were fascinated by the ancient Egyptians and used many of their symbols. Egyptians used snakes to represent change and life because snakes shed their old skin as they grow.
- Lotus: Lotus flowers represent rebirth. During the day, lotus flowers come out from the water where they grow. But at night, the flowers close and return to the water.
- Cedar of Lebanon: The cedar of Lebanon is an evergreen tree that can live for hundreds of years. It represents eternal life.

The design of Egyptian Avenue, a path of tombs at Highgate Cemetery that leads to the Circle of Lebanon, was inspired by ancient Egypt.

The Magnificent Seven were much grander than earlier graveyards. Their designs were inspired by many historic building styles. Part of the reason they were so magnificent, or grand, was because they had a social purpose too. In addition to visiting graves, people could take walks through the grounds, have picnics in the gardens, and more.

Each cemetery also had its own catacombs. These were exclusive and expensive. Only wealthy people could buy them. The early London catacombs were popular because they promised cleaner air and protected coffins. But they would turn out to be less perfect than they seemed.

CHAPTER 2
BEHIND CLOSED DOORS

A door to the Brompton Cemetery catacombs

Lead coffins were heavy! Some of the cemeteries had special elevators that gently lowered coffins from the funeral chapel to the catacombs beneath.

Coffins placed in catacombs were not covered in soil where they could naturally decay. So, to prevent leaks, they had an inner shell made of lead. This protected the body from pests too. Unfortunately, the heavy metal didn't work as well as people hoped.

Many coffins are still intact in the catacombs. But the wooden outsides have decayed, showing the lead underneath.

A Stinky Secret

Lead was supposed to stop leaks. But it didn't prevent bodies from decomposing. As bacteria broke down the body, stinky gases built up inside the coffin. Not every coffin could handle the pressure from these gases trying to escape. Sometimes the lead burst at the seams and released the smell into the catacombs.

DECLASSIFIED

In August 1865, a fire spread in the Kensal Green catacombs. Ten coffins caught fire. Five of them were almost completely destroyed.

Rumors quickly spread about how the fire started. Firefighters found a pile of coal and rags in a corner nearby. But the items weren't burned. Someone had also reported seeing smoke coming from the same vault two weeks earlier. Were the incidents connected? Investigators thought it might have been an accident. Perhaps the flame of a candle used during a recent burial caught on the dry wood of an old coffin.

Whether it was an accident with a candle or something else, no one knows for sure what started the Kensal Green fire. The cemetery has taken this smoky secret to the grave.

Brompton's catacombs never completely filled.

Soon the catacombs had the same problems that the smelly city churchyards had. Some people claimed that lead coffin burials were unclean. They feared the catacombs could make visitors and workers sick. Would the catacombs cause another wave of disease?

Empty Shelves

Some people were against the catacombs soon after they were built. But many families chose to bury their loved ones there. Catacomb spaces at Highgate Cemetery sold so quickly that more catacombs were built there in 1876. The Kensal Green catacombs were also extremely popular. Strangely, the Brompton catacombs never came close to filling up. Only about five hundred of the thousands of spots there were ever sold.

SOLVE IT

////////////////////////////////////

In addition to its catacombs, a large, aboveground tomb stands in Brompton Cemetery. It's decorated with detailed images like strange wheels and a ring of holes. A mysterious inventor and an Egyptologist designed it for wealthy Londoner Hannah Courtoy, and some people think they might have built a time machine inside! But without a key, no one was able to enter for more than 150 years. What do you think? Is it possible the tomb could travel through time?

Hannah Courtoy's tomb at Brompton Cemetery

The elaborate buildings and gardens in the Magnificent Seven are expensive to maintain.

Late in the nineteenth century, a different mode of caring for the dead gained interest. Some people began to speak up for cremation, or the burning of dead bodies to turn them into ash. Bodies posed no health risk to the living as ash. A jar of ashes also took up much less space than a coffin.

Cremation became more popular. Many people were still concerned about how clean the catacombs were. Cemeteries and their catacombs were also expensive to maintain. Interest in the London catacombs began to fade.

The Magnificent Seven's catacombs began to close. Even though there were still open spots, Brompton stopped catacomb burials by 1915. Then the West Norwood and Nunhead Cemeteries performed their final catacomb burials in the 1930s. Had the London catacombs reached a dead end?

CHAPTER 3
DECAY AND RETURN

The West Norwood catacombs

A sign at Abney Park Cemetery warns visitors to stay out of buildings.

Warning: Keep Out

The London catacombs began to fall apart. Some were damaged by bombs during World War II (1939–1945). Still more were vandalized. Some of the cemeteries like Nunhead and Kensal Green sealed off parts of the catacombs to keep people safe and stop the spread of vandalism. The catacombs had once hidden decay. But now they were decaying themselves.

Risky Restorations

People began to take notice of the catacombs again in the mid-1900s. In the 1970s, groups began to stand up for preserving London's cemeteries and their catacombs. Some of the groups were successful. But public health was still a concern.

You might think that after more than one hundred years, the catacombs no longer pose a threat of disease. But while it is safe for tourists to visit the restored areas of the catacombs, workers must be very careful when restoring them. Lead coffins have been known to preserve a body's tissues like hair for hundreds of years. Deadly diseases like smallpox might be preserved too. What else might still be inside?

Tourists can only visit certain parts of the catacombs.

The Anglican Chapel at Nunhead Cemetery was destroyed by fire in 1976. But its ruins were made stable and are sometimes used for music and theater shows.

Visitors Underground

While much has been done to restore the surviving catacombs, they still have secrets. In the late 1960s, a story spread that a vampire ran loose in Highgate Cemetery and its catacombs. People reported finding animals drained of blood and seeing bodies rise from their graves. One man, David Farrant, even claimed to have seen a gray figure wandering the grounds! Crowds gathered at Highgate for a vampire hunt in early 1970. While no vampire was caught, some people still

Could a vampire run loose in Highgate Cemetery?

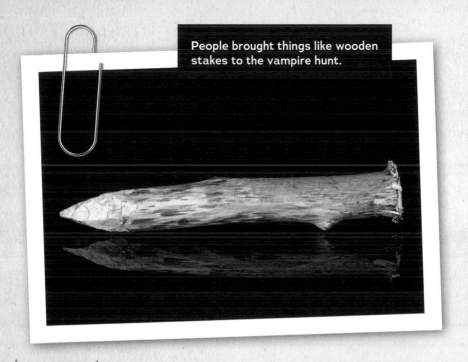

People brought things like wooden stakes to the vampire hunt.

wonder what might be living at Highgate Cemetery.

Although rumors about bloodthirsty creatures at the catacombs are rarer these days, the catacombs still have other mysteries. Vandals continue to harm the cemeteries. And in the 2000s, rumors spread that people were performing black magic in the Abney Park catacombs. This type of magic is thought to be dangerous or evil. What other secrets might the catacombs be hiding?

The mysterious London catacombs continue to interest locals and tourists alike. Some of the cemeteries like Kensal Green and West Norwood sometimes host tours through some of the catacombs' tunnels and vaults. The West

The City of London Cemetery and Crematorium offers burials in modern catacombs.

Norwood catacombs can even be used as a spooky spot to film videos!

But will the catacombs ever be revisited for their first purpose? London locals might be the first to find out. Although it wasn't part of the original Magnificent Seven, the City of London Cemetery and Crematorium was still offering catacomb burials as late as 2022. And more might be needed soon.

By 2022, England faced a burial crisis again. Cemeteries are running out of room. The debate about how and where to lay the dead to rest continues. Could modern catacombs be the answer? Maybe Brompton's empty shelves will finally be filled. Only time will tell.

Timeline

1832: A cholera pandemic reaches London, leading to thousands of deaths.

1833: Kensal Green Cemetery, the first of the Magnificent Seven, opens.

1876: More catacombs are built at Highgate Cemetery.

1915: Brompton Cemetery catacombs have their last burial.

1970: A vampire hunt takes place at Highgate Cemetery.

1970s: Friends of the cemeteries, groups who wanted to preserve the Magnificent Seven cemeteries and catacombs, begin forming.

1997: A coffin elevator in one of the Kensal Green catacombs is restored.

2022: The City of London catacombs continue offering burial spaces.

England is running out of burial space again.

Glossary

chapel: a building, room, or place for prayer or special religious services like funerals

crisis: an emergency

decay: the breakdown of tissues like skin after death

decompose: to break down or rot

population: the number of people or animals that live in a certain place

preserving: keeping or saving from injury, loss, or ruin

reform: to change things for the better

represent: to be a sign or symbol of something

restore: to fix something to return it to its original condition

vandalize: to destroy or damage property such as buildings on purpose

Victorians: people who lived during the Victorian era (1820–1914), a historical period named for Queen Victoria of England who ruled between 1837–1901

Learn More

Britannica Kids: Catacomb
https://kids.britannica.com/kids/article/catacomb/399915

Britannica Kids: Vampire
https://kids.britannica.com/kids/article/vampire/600681

Epidemiology Facts for Kids
https://easyscienceforkids.com/epidemiology/

Gottschall, Meghan. *Rituals and Traditions*. Fremont, CA: Full Tilt, 2020.

Hutchison, Patricia. *Explore London*. Mankato, MN: 12-Story Library, 2020.

Hyde, Natalie. *Ancient Underground Structures*. New York: Crabtree, 2019.

Kerry, Isaac. *Inside King Tut's Tomb*. Minneapolis: Lerner Publications, 2023.

Magnificent Seven Cemeteries Facts for Kids
https://kids.kiddle.co/Magnificent_Seven_cemeteries

Index

Photo Acknowledgments

Image credits: Peter Phipp/Getty Images, p. 1; Scott Wylie/Wikimedia Commons (CC BY 2.0), p. 5; RMAX/Getty Images, p. 6; HeritageDaily/Wikimedia Commons (CC BY 3.0), pp. 7, 16, 22; © Roberto Conte/Getty Images, p. 8; Morphart Creation/Shutterstock, p. 9; Luke Abrahams/Getty Images, p. 11; Andrea Pucci/ Getty Images, p. 13; Colors Hunter - Chasseur de Couleurs/Getty Images, p. 14; TylaArabas/Getty Images, p. 15; Simon Burchell/Wikimedia Commons (CC BY-SA 4.0), p. 18; Edwardx/Wikimedia Commons (CC BY-SA 4.0), p. 19; Robert Stainforth/Alamy Stock Photo, p. 20; Maria Jefferis/Alamy Stock Photo, p. 23; Guy Corbishley/Alamy Stock Photo, p. 24; Stefano Ravera/Alamy Stock Photo, p. 25; mango2friendly/Getty Images, p. 26; Yevhenii Orlov/Getty Images, p. 27; Acabashi/Wikimedia Commons (CC BY-SA 4.0), p. 28.

Design elements: Ivan Gromov/Unsplash; Marjan Blan/Unsplash; fotograzia/ Getty Images; Reddavebatcave/Shutterstock; AVS-Images/Shutterstock.

Cover: kentaylordesign/Shutterstock.